WORD FROM ROME:
The Pilgrimage

BY REV. STEPHEN GRUNOW
&
JOSEPH GLOOR

Photography by Joseph Gloor

Copyright © 2019 by Word on Fire Catholic Ministries

All rights reserved
Published by Word on Fire

LCCN 2019902555

First Edition

Preface

Friends, throughout the month of October 2018, I had the privilege of joining my brother bishops and the Holy Father for the Synod on Young People, the Faith, and Vocational Discernment. It was my first time attending a synod, and it was quite an adventure!

During my time in Rome, I asked Word on Fire's CEO Fr. Steve Grunow and Producer Joseph Gloor to take Word on Fire viewers on a virtual pilgrimage to the holy sites of the Eternal City, capturing not only the history and splendor of these places but also their spiritual depth. With help from Manny Marquez of Remuda Pictures, the project came to life, and the result was a beautiful eleven-part series on some of the most spectacular places in Rome.

What you hold in your hands is a visual reproduction of the entire miniseries, based on the insightful dialogues from the video series and exquisite photography from our Producer. We wanted you to experience this extraordinary pilgrimage in book form—something you can store on your shelf, return to again and again, and perhaps even lend to a friend to read. However, for those who prefer the video format (or would prefer to use the two together), we're also including a DVD copy of *The Pilgrimage*, which you can find on the inside pocket of this book.

Thank you to my Word on Fire team for your hard work and support throughout the month of October, and to every person who joined us—or who is about to join us—on this Roman journey.

God bless you!

Peace,

+ Robert Barron

Bishop Robert Barron

There's No Faith Like Rome's

by Matthew Becklo

Religion in the twenty-first century West—when it is practiced at all—is more and more marked by two interlocking qualities: splintering and subjectivity. The major religions have splintered into various denominations; those denominations have further splintered into sub-denominations; the sub-denominations have splintered into different branches, factions, and expressions; and so on. This splintering has sharpened—and been sharpened by—the Enlightenment emphasis on the autonomous individual, which tends to relegate religious truth to a subjective choice and religious faith to subjective experience.

Today, the choices are multiplied—and the chooser magnified—like never before. And yet many young people are opting out of religion entirely for a new age syncretism of spiritualities, or (more and more the case) simply opting out of spirituality altogether. This is precisely why the Roman Catholic Church continues to captivate, mystify, and allure so many people, even (and especially) today. Against this backdrop, Catholicism just looks...*strange*. I recently came to see this aspect of the Church in a whole new light after visiting Rome for the first time.

Like many Catholics, I've seen images of St. Peter's Basilica throughout my life. But I never really imagined I would ever go there or what it might be like. Shortly after arriving in Rome, I set out on foot to St. Peter's Square, and what I realized very quickly was that its size and scope far exceeded anything I had ever pictured. It's a vast, wide open space, a kind of cobblestone valley bordered by Bernini's colonnades and pulled slightly uphill—as if by a kind of gravitational field—toward the mountainous, ornate façade of the basilica.

But as overwhelming as the square was, it paled in comparison to the interior of the church, which I saw a few days later. It was hard to accept that fallen human minds and hands were responsible for such sprawling grandeur; it looked more like the handiwork of angels or aliens. The size alone is dizzying, but every square inch of it also radiates design, intelligibility, beauty, and power. It was an impossibly big, bold, and beautiful proclamation; and yet there it was, the whole thing consecrated to God for his glory.

St. Peter's is not a subjective matter. It's not an inner perspective or feeling that one can grasp, turn over in the mind, and take or leave. Instead, it's more like Jean-Luc Marion's "saturated phenomenon": something so vast and visible and "given" that it seizes the mind trying to frame it. It is an incarnate reality—a particular church, in a particular city, with a particular history—and it is unabashedly and stubbornly *there*.

But while the art and architecture of Rome conveys the dense objectivity of our faith, it also conveys its unity down through history. Catholicism is finally rooted not in Renaissance extravagance or medieval Scholasticism, but in the Scripture and Tradition of the earliest centuries of Christianity. John Henry Newman famously remarked that to be to be deep in history is to cease to be Protestant—precisely because to be deep in Christian history is to be deep in Catholic history. And while Catholic doctrine has certainly developed down the ages (another famous observation of Newman's), its fundamentals have remained the same. This isn't a faith that splinters under the weight of political, social, cultural, moral, spiritual, or intellectual shifts; it's an ark as sturdy as rock.

If this unity is remarkable just in light of how old the Church is, it's all the more remarkable in light of how many attacks it has endured. Peter and Paul came to spread the good news of Jesus Christ's saving death and resurrection to pagan Rome—and they paid for it. The fisherman was crucified upside down in the circus of Nero and buried right on the very spot where St. Peter's Basilica now stands. It took some very bloody centuries for Christianity to go from a dangerous, ragtag movement in the shadows of the Palatine Hill to the official religion of Rome. Even when these outside threats faded (and in fact, they very much remain today, with more Christians dying for their faith in the twentieth century

than in all the previous centuries combined), the Church has always been plagued by inside threats—namely, the evil actions of some of its members and even some of its leaders. The Church's history is riddled with Catholics doing horrible things—executions, persecution, corruption, interdictions, simony, hypocrisy—behavior that by all accounts should've consigned the Church to the ash heap of history. And yet it has lasted—and not only lasted, but spread like wildfire to the ends of the earth.

It seems reasonable to conclude that the planting of the Church in the Eternal City in the first century, and the flowering and fortitude of the Church in the centuries after, are not just accidents of history. The blood of the apostles and martyrs nurtured the Gospel of peace in Rome, and through Rome, cities all over the world—even as humanity (and behind humanity, hell) threw its worst at the Church, from both inside and out. Doesn't this bear witness to the divine origin of its mission, the explosive truth of its message, the transformative witness of its saints?

During the Mass for the canonization of Pope Paul VI, Oscar Romero,

and five other holy men and women, I looked down on the successor of Peter and a slow, stately procession of bishops from around the world, and I was struck by something else: all those centuries and all those popes, running from St. Peter's burial to the present moment with Pope Francis in St. Peter's Square—and there I was, looking right at it, breathing in the same air, participating in the same reality. This was not a museum or an archive or a reenactment. The Church may be as solid and ancient as stone, but it's a *living* stone. The Catholic faith has great breadth and depth, but it's a vibrant breadth, a rushing depth—like a mighty river making its way through history to eternity. Every Catholic alive today is swept up in its life and commissioned to make disciples of all nations. The Church does not have this mission; it *is* this mission.

And the mission lives on.

The Palatine Hill

There's no better place to start this Roman pilgrimage than Palatine Hill, which is the centermost of the seven hills of Rome. The hill stands above the Roman Forum on one side and the Circus Maximus on the other. Roman civilization has its origins on Palatine Hill, and excavations show people lived in the area since the tenth century BC. Since the time of Augustus, the emperors made this hill their home.

Palatine Hill was like the centerpiece of a wheel, with all of the spokes of Roman civilization turning around it—religion, culture, politics, economics. Hills, especially the seven hills of Rome, were also indicative of a place where heaven and earth meet. Therefore, though the Roman Empire had spread across the entire Mediterranean, Palatine Hill was a place of special significance.

When the Old Testament came to its fruition with the arrival of Christ, this great empire also had control over the lands of the Israelites. But as the Book of Revelation ends, it predicts the triumph of the Lamb (Christ) over Babylon (Rome). And it actually happened! There was a great transition in Roman culture, and Rome became the means by which the Church expanded out into the world. Today, Rome is no longer the city of the Caesars; it's the city of the Apostle Peter and his successor. We can see the remains of the once magnificent

palaces of the Caesars today, but the Caesars are all dust in their graves.

Remember that there is always a conflict between God and the empires, between Caesar and Christ. As Bishop Barron explains in *The Priority of Christ*, this conflict already emerges in Luke's infancy narrative, which contrasts the safety and comfort of the mighty Augustus' palace on Palatine Hill—"the site from which the census decree undoubtedly went

out"—with the vulnerable, primitive hostel in Bethlehem sheltering two ordinary travelers: Joseph and Mary. "*Kyrios* Jesus has begun his battle, in short, with *kyrios* Augustus; a tale of competing kingdoms, competing conceptions of power, is being told."

Augustus fell into the dust of his grave, but there's always a world order that seeks to impose its power and will upon humanity. Yet this ragtag band of the followers of the Galilean managed to

survive all the empires as they rise and fall and come and go. At times it seems the Church is rising in glory; at times it seems oppressed and small. But it continues to make its way through history.

And this is why we begin our Roman pilgrimage where Rome began. Because in the providence of God, it was from this imperial hill that Peter and Paul took the Catholic faith out into the whole world.

The Basilica of St. Bartholomew

The Basilica of St. Bartholomew was founded in 998 AD, and contains the relics of the Apostle Bartholomew. This beautiful church also houses memorials to the Christian martyrs of the twentieth and twenty-first centuries. The caretaker of the basilica is the Community of Sant'Egidio, an ecumenical Catholic movement whose guiding ethos is prayer, care for the poor, and the promotion of peace among all people.

St. Bartholomew was one of the Twelve Apostles of Christ. After the Resurrection, Paul went west, but Bartholomew went east, even getting as far as India. His hagiography says that he died a martyr's death by being flayed—or skinned—alive.

The brutal martyrdom of St. Bartholomew was immortalized in Michelangelo's "Last Judgment" fresco of the Sistine Chapel. In the *Michelangelo* episode of *The Pivotal Players*, Bishop Barron points out the image of St. Bartholomew, located at Christ's lower right, while examining the fresco. "Go to the top left, and come right down through the judging arm of Jesus, and then across his body to St. Bartholomew....Look what he's holding; he's holding his flayed skin. That's how he was martyred...but the skin, as everyone points out, has the face of Michelangelo. It's a distorted self-portrait."

Why is martyrdom at the heart of Christianity? Because Christianity doesn't just make claims about metaphysics. It makes claims about the true ruler of the world: the Lord Jesus. That's what made Cesar nervous

in the first century; that's what made tyrants like Hitler nervous in the twentieth century; and that's what makes the great powers of the world nervous about Christianity all the time. Christianity is like an explosive device, a powder keg, that's been set into cultures. It can dramatically overturn things and change things by declaring a greater power to whom humanity owes its allegiance. At times, that can explode into martyrdom.

And the blood of the martyrs, as Tertullian said, is the seed of the Church. The great mystery of divine providence in history is that when things seem to be going really, really wrong with the Church, somehow God turns the situation around in an extraordinary way. As martyrdom is happening, as people are being killed, it seems impossible that Christianity would ever bounce back. But inevitably, over time, that's precisely what happens.

What you see very clearly in a martyr like Bartholomew is that the Church is not a self-help program. Rather, the Church is a divine summons to humanity, from Christ, to be incorporated into the mystical extension of his Incarnation across space and time. And because it is the missionary Body of Christ, this summons will involve suffering and oftentimes persecution—but that suffering is always fruitful, and always redemptive.

The Church of St. Mary in the Valley

St. Mary of the Valley is one of the grandest of the baroque churches of Rome. It is the home of the Oratory of St. Philip Neri. The original church was built by St. Gregory the Great, and in 1575, Pope Gregory XIII gave the church property to St. Phillip Neri. Over time, through the generosity of donors and patrons, the magnificent church you see today was built and embellished, its beauty foreshadowing the glory of heaven.

Philip Neri is known as the Third Apostle of Rome (after Saints Peter and Paul). When he came to Rome at eighteen years old, he was a layman who successfully dealt with the desuetude and decline of the Catholic faith there. His strategy was to evangelize through one-on-one, face-to-face encounters, engaging in a conversation about the faith and then presenting practical opportunities to assist the poor. This led to the grander vision of the

Oratory movement, which involved bringing people together for a spiritual talk—like a sermon or a homily—and to enjoy the lively music of the age. After the experience of the talk and the music, Neri would invite the people to the sacrament of Reconciliation, and then through that doorway, lead them back into the Church. So while the Mass was not the starting point of the Oratory movement, it was the ultimate goal.

Many young people today become attracted to Christian life through nondenominational churches that mirror the Oratory movement by offering spiritual guidance, a fun and entertaining environment, and a sense of community. But the problem is this: these churches and these gatherings never lead anywhere greater, and when life becomes difficult and forces difficult questions, they become irrelevant. You can get sermons on podcasts; you can get music on your phone or at a concert; and you can get community at a barbeque!

But you can only get the Eucharist—the source and summit of the Christian life—at the Mass. Christ wants people to have the sacraments, and Neri was using a hook or an invitation to bring people to them. But he knew that they would have to pass through something in order to get there. He would have to prepare them; and he found an effective way to do that.

There is a pressing need today to re-evangelize Rome and all of the Western world in the spirit of St. Philip Neri. This is what Word on Fire hopes to do as it expands from a ministry into a movement, and it's what we as Catholic Christians should be doing all the time.

The Church of St. Mary of the Mount

St. Mary of the Mount is a beautiful, baroque, jewel box of a church tucked inside the city center of Rome near the Colosseum. The church was built in 1580 to house an image of the Blessed Virgin Mary. St. Mary of the Mount is associated with many saints, including St. Paul of the Cross, St. Alphonsus Ligouri, and St. Vincent Pallotti. The body of St. Benedict Joseph Labre is reverently entombed in this church, and his shrine provides a prayerful respite for pilgrims from around the world.

Benedict Joseph Labre was a Frenchman born in 1748. He discerned that he had a religious calling, but when he tried to be a priest, he failed, and when he tried to become a monk, he also failed—multiple times. Labre discerned that God had chosen him for a mission of poverty, pilgrimage, and penance. So he left his small village in France and began to make his way to Rome. He visited all the great pilgrimage sites and shrines on his way,

living by the generosity of others and essentially becoming homeless.

In the plan of God, this wandering pilgrim made a lasting impression on the city of Rome. He was known for his extraordinary prayer and holiness, as well as his generosity—oddly enough—towards the poor. He would receive, and then he would give away. Within months after his death, people began to report miraculous cures through his heavenly intercession. To

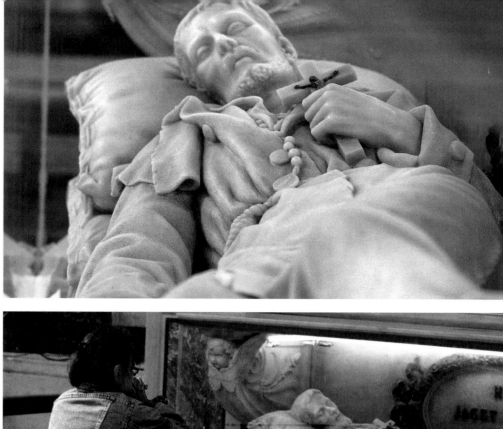

this day he is honored as a friend to the people of Rome, and Labre's shrine in St. Mary of the Mount is surrounded by little notes left by visiting pilgrims.

Many young people who are not yet married and have not entered the religious life wonder: Do I even have a purpose in life? Do I have a calling that will finally make me happy? Others are convinced that they will be happy when they achieve or get some material goal or success. But Labre didn't have a spouse or children, a religious vocation, a house, or a job; and yet he found the great happiness of his own unique mission from God.

In accounts of Labre's life, people said that they rarely heard him speak. We all have something to say, and we all want to be heard. But Labre took a different path: rather than speaking, he was listening, and what he was listening for was the voice of God.

In doing so, he spoke volumes about who God is and what it looks like to be a follower of Christ.

Remember the beautiful Philippians hymn: "He emptied himself, taking the form of a slave...he humbled himself, becoming obedient to death, even death on a cross." That is the Christian life in all of its radicality. Empty yourself. Take the lowest place. Go low so you can go high.

The Basilica of St. Sabina

The Basilica of St. Sabina is an ancient church located on the Aventine Hill. It is the oldest complete church in Rome built in the basilica style, preserving the original design and simplicity of decoration. The church is dedicated to the martyr St. Sabina, a Roman noblewoman who gave up her life rather than deny Christ and his Church. Magnificent carved panels on the wooden doors at the entrance of the basilica include what many believe to be the earliest depiction of the crucifixion of the Lord Jesus. The Basilica of St. Sabina is the mother church of—and still cared for by—the Dominican Order, and the priory adjacent to the church is the home of the International Dominican Community.

Dominic, the founder of the Dominican Order, was born in 1170. There is a story that his mother had a dream, when Dominic was still in the womb, that she was giving birth to a dog with a torch in his mouth, and the dog went running out of the house and set the whole world on fire. Thus, his name Dominic: *Dominus* (Lord) and *canis* (the hound of the Lord). Dominic eventually encountered a resurgent sect of gnostics, a heretical group called the Cathars, and he engaged them in dialogue. He realized that the Church needed a new movement or community to deal with this resurgent gnosticism, and the Order of Preachers was founded, eventually receiving papal approval in 1217.

But then Dominic shifted the mission; he decided to send his men

into the cities. The Gospel was not being adequately proclaimed in these rising, urban centers of medieval life—particularly in universities. At the time, the Dominicans were viewed as off-putting and strange, even radical. What were these priests doing out of monasteries? What were they doing out of their parishes? But that was their mission...and it worked. Within less than a generation, there were Dominicans in all the major cities of Europe.

Over time, the Church can become ossified. It can become preoccupied with its institutions, and caught up in ad intra conversations that are only of concern to Church insiders. But the Holy Spirit responds by raising up new movements—not only of teachers and preachers but of witnesses. Dominic inaugurated a movement of teaching and preaching to combat the spread of heresy. But he also saw the need to go out into the culture, boldly moving into those spaces where preaching the Gospel would have the greatest impact.

It's undeniable that a certain measure of ossification has happened in the Church today. But perhaps this is what is happening right now in the life of the Church. Could the Holy Spirit be raising up teachers and preachers who are willing to go out into the culture, proclaim the Gospel, and invite people into the unique Christian way of life?

The Church of St. Agnes in Agone

The church of St. Agnes in Agone overlooks the Piazza Navona, one of the premier public spaces in the city of Rome. Inside the church, there are monumental bas-reliefs depicting the Holy Family over the main altar. A statue of St. Agnes, the heavenly patron of the church, looms over her side altar. The skull of St. Agnes is reverently displayed in a small, austere chapel, the simplicity of which stands in stark contrast to the rest of the church, but effectively communicates the gravity of St. Agnes' self-sacrifice.

Agnes died in 304 at just thirteen years old. Her family was Roman nobility, and a potential suitor whom Agnes had scorned reported her family as Christians to the local magistrate. Christianity was becoming more and more influential in the Empire, and the authorities were increasingly concerned about the resulting political shift. The thirteen-year-old Agnes may not have been a mighty revolutionary figure, but she was the daughter of Roman nobility, and the authorities wanted to show in the

most dramatic way that Christians would be punished.

Agnes was arrested and put on trial, and because she would not reject her faith, she was convicted. Both law and custom dictated that she could not be executed until she was deflowered. So she was stripped naked and paraded in the street, taken to a brothel where she was likely raped, and because the pyre prepared for her wouldn't burn, either stabbed in the throat or beheaded. For any person of any age

to endure the torture of this state-sponsored terrorism is incredible, and not surprisingly, people immediately began to reverence this young girl.

All love demands sacrifice, and Agnes' death was an act of great love. We often conceive of martyrdom as a political act against the establishment, an act of conscience in the face of tyranny. Martyrdom is usually those things, but it is also an act of love for Christ and the Church. Out of a profound inner love for what Christ did—giving his life for Agnes—Agnes gave her life for Christ. She discerned that this was what Christ was asking her to do, trusted that the suffering would be, like Christ's, redemptive suffering—and accepted it.

Could you accept a calling that cost you your entire life? Oftentimes we mistakenly treat a vocation as pinpointing what we want and then receiving divine sanction for it. But this is usually the wrong decision, and deep down most of us know that. God is the one who chooses the mission. Our choice in relation to that choice—*his* choice—is whether we accept it or not.

But how do we know our mission? St. John of the Cross gives us this encouraging (and devastating) advice: if it's difficult, it's likely what God wants us to do. We have to break the ego, turn toward the cross of Jesus, and say, "I'm all in." That is the call of Christian discipleship: take up your cross and follow him.

The Church of St. Ignatius of Loyola

The Church of St. Ignatius is a stunning masterpiece of baroque art and architecture. Of particular note is the church's decorated ceiling, upon which a painted riot of colors and sumptuous figures dazzle the eyes with dramatic compositions and illusions of perspective. A multitude of magnificent side chapels celebrate Catholic spirituality, culminating in the grand high altar. The story of St. Ignatius is told in paintings and sculptures throughout the church—a fitting tribute to the founder of the Jesuits and heavenly patron of this church. The church is also the resting place for numerous Jesuit luminaries and saints, including St. Aloysius Gonzaga.

Aloysius Gonzaga was born in 1568, the eldest son of one of the wealthiest noble houses of Europe. His family was politically, economically, and religiously connected. But Gonzaga decided to eschew it all—title, position, prerogatives, power—to enter a life of poverty and obedience in the Jesuit order. His family, of course, opposed the decision.

By 1591, a horrible plague came to Rome, and Aloysius Gonzaga and the young members of the Jesuit community were sent out into the streets to minister to the victims. Gonzaga ended up catching the disease himself and dying.

The Gospel exposes us to risk and makes us vulnerable. It takes us out on an adventure, but it doesn't give us certainty in terms of the outcome. It also changes our perception of value in relation to the world. In every age, young people

are enamored by the glittering images of worldly cultures: celebrity, success, money, power, honors. We absolutize these things; we make them into our gods and follow them. But the Gospel declares these gods to be false. There is one true God that we can follow, and his name is Jesus Christ. When we embrace that message, our perceptions and desires change, and our lives are radically reoriented. It happened to Aloysius Gonzaga, and it happens to those who hear the call of the Gospel in every age of the Church's life.

The Gospel is not about settling on the easiest common denominator just to get by. It's a call to heroic virtue, which is what being a saint is. And sanctity is far greater a possibility if we take the lowest place, away from worldly wealth and power. We tend to qualify that, trying to live vicariously through the saints instead of aspiring to be saints ourselves. But that possibility, which is a God-given grace, is not just something that was given to Aloysius Gonzaga. It's given to everyone.

Listen to the Gospel for what it says, and respond to it for what it is. And look to the lives of the saints, who show us the form of discipleship. Being a disciple doesn't look like our culture of celebrity and success, a culture fixated on the glittering images that rise and fall and come and go. It looks like an intent focus on what Jesus wants for you.

Basilica of St. Paul Outside the Walls

The Basilica of St. Paul Outside the Walls was built by the Emperor Constantine to enshrine the burial site of St. Paul the Apostle. It was consecrated in the year 324. The monumental basilica you see today was built in the nineteenth century, as the church was destroyed by a fire in 1823. Underneath the altar, the tomb of the Apostle Paul remains in tact. The interior of the basilica is lavishly decorated. Everywhere the glint of gold and colorful varieties of marble and other precious stones catch the eye and evoke the glory of

heaven. A frieze runs along the top of the interior walls depicting all the popes from St. Peter to his current successor, Pope Francis.

Paul was a persecutor of the Church and an enemy of Christ who became Christ's greatest friend. He was a witness to the Resurrection; he was an apostle, a teacher, an evangelist, a missionary; and probably most importantly, he is the spiritual progenitor of all Christians—indeed, Christianity—in the West. He created the template

from which all the missionary energy, verve, and vigor of the Church emanates out through history.

As Bishop Barron writes in *Catholicism*: "Paul realized that his mission was to declare to everybody—Jew and Gentile alike—that they had a new king....The second half of the Acts of the Apostles tells the story of Saul (now called Paul) scurrying furiously around Asia Minor, Palestine, Greece, and Italy for around twenty years proclaiming this Lordship of Jesus."

Paul went out proclaiming "Christ and him crucified." His preaching is kerygmatic, which means that it was about Jesus himself, and what he accomplished through his life, death, and resurrection. And while cultures and the concerns of different ages come and go, that message is the same yesterday, today, and forever.

To be a missionary like Paul doesn't mean we have to paddle down the Amazon in a canoe or go to some other far-off place. If you are a bap-tized Christian, you are a missionary. Friends, family, people who are known to you, unknown to you—you're called to go out into the culture, introducing people to Christ and inviting them into his Church. This can be a scary thing to do. But everything worth doing in life involves great risk, difficulty, and struggle. What good is an easy Christianity?

We now have an established, insti-tutionalized Church with beautiful buildings all over the world. But it's never a given that people will come to our institutions or be evangelized by them. In fact, for every one person that joins the Catholic Church today, six are leaving. We have to make the Pauline move of going out into the culture and drawing people in. Paul used the state-of-the-art technolo-gy available to him at the time—the Roman roads—to do that. We have the digital roads of the internet—and if St. Paul had the internet, you can bet he would have used it for the Gospel!

The Archbasilica of St. John Lateran

The Archbasilica of St. John Lateran is the cathedral church of the diocese of Rome. It is dedicated to Christ the savior and is under the heavenly patronage of St. John the Baptist and St. John the Evangelist. The original basilica was built by the Emperor Constantine on land he donated to the Church for the purpose of creating not only a fitting place for Christian worship but also a residence for the pope, the Bishop of Rome. The Lateran Basilica is the most ancient and revered of all the basilicas of Rome, and right on the front is its ancient title: "Mother and Head of All the Churches of the World."

The importance of the Lateran Basilica largely stems from its designation as the pope's see church. "See" is from the Latin *sedes*, meaning chair. In Greek, the word is *cathedra* (giving us the word "cathedral"). The pope comes here on a regular basis for various celebrations. And right in the back of the church, you can see the beautiful *cathedra*—literally the pope's chair—from which his teaching goes forth.

The Lateran Basilica is also a great apostolic church. Monumental statues of the Apostles line the central aisle, almost like they are pillars of the Church itself. But of particular importance to the church are St. John (to whom the church is dedicated) and St. Paul and St. Peter (whose skulls rest in the impressive reliquary above the main altar). These three represent the three great offices of the Church:

the Johannine (the prayerful, liturgical, and mystical), the Pauline (teaching, preaching, and evangelizing), and the Petrine (rule and governance). In other words, the priestly, the prophetic, and the kingly.

Every baptized person has the priestly responsibility of praying for the living and the dead, praying for their family, and above all, coming to Mass. The Mass is not like a theater event where we sit in the chairs and take it in. Lay people are participating in the Mass precisely as *priest*—not as ordained priests but in the priestly office of praying in union with the priest. The fact that so many Catholics now stay away from the Mass is a terrible thing because they're not fulfilling this priestly calling.

Every baptized person is also meant to be a prophet. We are meant to preach and teach and proclaim the faith. When baptized Catholics keep quiet about the faith and allow the voice of the world to echo, they are not living up to this prophetic calling.

And every baptized person is kingly. You have a kingly responsibility for your own soul and body; to some degree, you have a kingly responsibility over some aspect of God's creation, whether through family, work, etc.; and you have a kingly responsibility to lead people to the kingdom of God. If you are baptized, you are therefore priest, prophet, and king—and the three great Apostles of the Lateran Basilica are guides for you.

CHRISTO · SALVATORI ·

CLEMENS · XII · PONT · MAX · ANNO · V · ... N · HON · SS · IOAN · BAPT · ET · EVAN ·

The Basilica of St. Clement

The Basilica of St. Clement is not the grandest of the churches of Rome, but it is richly decorated and exceptionally interesting. Pilgrims descend into the church from the modern street level, entering a twelfth-century basilica. From there, they can descend further into the excavations beneath the church to explore the fourth-century precursor to the current basilica, and even further to a Roman street from the first century AD. The Basilica of St. Clement is dedicated to one of the earliest successors of St. Peter, and his relics are interred under the main altar.

The glittering mosaic in the apse depicts the cross of our Lord Jesus as an abundant tree of life, inviting pilgrims to contemplate the mystery of Christ's death as a source of creativity and hope. The cross of Jesus isn't just simply about Jesus' death; it's also about the emergence of a new form of life, which is life in Christ. The mosaic reminds us of Jesus' words from the Gospel of John: "I am the vine, you are the branches." This is dramatically displayed in all its facets and forms. Animals, plants, people, earthly things, heavenly things—all of it is included in Christ's new life.

The Basilica of St. Clement is really more of a time machine than a church. You walk through layers and layers of history, from a first

century temple to the pagan gods (the street level that Peter and Paul would have walked), to the fourth century (when Christianity was no longer persecuted), to the twelfth century (when this beautiful basilica was built), and finally to the modern street level. Young people visiting St. Clement see—in one place—the Church moving through time, going from very small to very grand, from persecuted to established.

But the Church never belongs to just one generation or one point in time. There is an eternal reality to the Church because it is ultimately the extension of the Incarnation across space and time—the living, moving, breathing Body of Christ in the world today. It is given to our generation as a gift to share among ourselves, but our purpose is to then create a new generation of Christians to whom we pass that reality on. We are history-minded and future-oriented.

The Church brings forth all that is good from the past, bears it into the present, and delivers it as a gift to the future. In a thousand years, some space age church might be built on top of this basilica, because the Church continues to build on itself; and like Christ himself, it is ancient and forever new. As Bishop Barron says, there is a "Grandma's attic" quality to Catholicism. We never throw anything away—and we don't keep anyone out.

The Basilica of St. Mary in Trastevere

The Basilica of St. Mary in Trastevere, established by Pope St. Callistus around 220 AD, is one of the oldest churches in Rome. The apse of the sanctuary gleans with the gold and sparkling colors of a thirteenth-century mosaic depicting the glorification of Christ's mother in heaven. The Holy Virgin is draped in the jewels and raiment of a Byzantine Empress, and Christ tenderly draws her close to his side. Beneath the scene are beautiful representations of highlights from

her life. The exterior of the basilica seems to keep a careful maternal watch over a graceful public square, beckoning pilgrims into a sanctuary of prayer and peace.

Consider four great scenes from the life of Mary, the first being the Annunciation. A heavenly visitor comes to an impoverished young girl and makes this stunning request of her: that she agree to be the mother of God. Imagine what was going through her mind! But this is what a

vocation is like. God asks something of us, and we have to make a decision.

The second is the wedding feast at Cana. Christ is invited to a wedding banquet, and the host runs out of wine. The mother of God intervenes and says to the servants: "Do whatever he tells you." Then Jesus turns jars of water into the finest wine. Mary's poignant line is not just a message for that particular situation. It's a message for us all. It's *her* message.

The third is the cross. Remove the saccharine piety from this scene: here is a woman who just watched her son tortured and killed. She might have had an intimation from the Old Testament that the Messiah would be a suffering servant… but *this*? Yet, in the midst of that incredible darkness, she trusts. We oftentimes think of faith as emotional security or good feelings. But faith most often looks like that disposition of the mother of God at the foot of the cross.

The fourth is Pentecost. Mary was situated among the Apostles as the Spirit descends upon them, giving them all of Christ's gifts. This indicates that the mother of God is always an active, living agent in the life of the Church. She who gave birth to the Son of God is there at the birth of the Church, and she is always where his disciples are gathered. This is why there are so many churches dedicated to her, and why so many people down the centuries have turned to her as a friend in times of trouble.

Listen to the great Magnificat, Mary's song of praise and thanksgiving: "He who is mighty has done great things for me, and holy is his name." God has "lifted up the lowly." Mary is the example of that *par excellence*. This woman, who during her lifetime would have walked the streets of the world unknown and been seen by many as a nonperson, is now Queen of Heaven and Earth!

The Catacombs
by Bishop Robert Barron

What a spiritual privilege it was to visit and say Mass in the Catacombs of Saints Callixtus, where many of the early popes and martyrs are buried. In 199, Callixtus was appointed superintendent of this Christian cemetery—likely the first bit of land ever owned by the Church—on the Appian Way. He became Bishop of Rome in 217 and died as a martyr about five years later, possibly during a riot against Christians.

Christians have always felt an attraction for these dark and chthonic places: whether it was the early believers hiding in the catacombs of Rome, or Sts. Jerome, Antony, Benedict, and Ignatius of Loyola fleeing to caves in order to pray, or visitors to Lourdes swarming into a massive underground basilica. Perhaps the attraction is rooted in Christmas, the day when the Son of God was born, as Chesterton put it, in a cave under the earth; or maybe it comes from Good Friday, the day when Christ was placed in a tomb hewn from the rock. Whatever the source, it remains true that when Christians venture into these sacred underground places, they don't feel threatened or claustrophobic, but at home, almost as though they are in the embrace of a mother.

The catacombs in particular remind us that our mother the Church is a persecuted Church. From Stephen, Peter, Paul, and all the martyrs of the early Church, to Charles Lwanga and Edith Stein, to the ordinary Christians in the twenty-first century who routinely risk their lives simply by declaring their faith and worshiping according to their lights.

the community of Jesus Christ has been the focus of the world's violence. The Church will announce, until the end of time, that the old world is passing away, that a new world of love, nonviolence, and life is emerging. This announcement always infuriates the world of sin. Always.

But in bringing us face-to-face with the ancient Christian custom of veneration of relics and bodies of the saints, the catacombs also remind us of the amazing grace of the Incarnation. How often, John Henry Newman

observed, we hear stories of believers placing napkins and cloths at the feet of martyrs to catch some of their blood, or of the reverence paid to the bones of the heroic dead in the catacombs, or of relics of saints working miracles. Such pious gestures are a logical development of the doctrine of the Incarnation. In Jesus Christ, the Word of God truly became *flesh*. He lived, died, and rose in a real human body, his life being placed in the bodies of the faithful through the materiality of the sacraments. And this, Newman realized, is why the Mystical Body of

the Church has, from the beginning, reverenced the bodies of the saints and treasured their relics. She has known that, as Paul put it, our bodies are temples of the Holy Spirit, dwelling places of Christ.

In the quiet, somber space of the catacombs, the pilgrim communes with those early popes and martyrs, leaving behind the luminous glories of Rome's churches above. And somehow, oddly, this is the whole point—an appropriate final destination of the pilgrimage.

IN MEMORY OF EDITH CECILIA McBRIDE

Saint Peter's Square

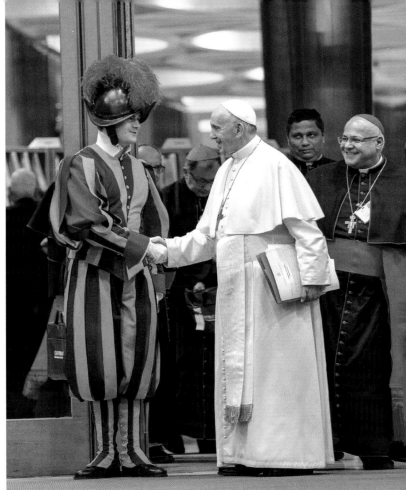